EAT.
PLAY.
LOVE.

LIFE LESSONS FROM MY DOG

Illustrated by EMMA BLOCK

THE EXPERIMENT

NEW YORK

EAT. PLAY. LOVE.: *Life Lessons from My Dog*
Illustrations copyright © 2019 by Emma Block
Text copyright © 2019 by Michael O'Mara Books Ltd.

Originally published in Great Britain as *Life Lessons I Learned from My Dog*
by LOM ART, an imprint of Michael O'Mara Books Ltd., in 2019.
First published in North America in revised form by The Experiment, LLC, in 2019.

The Experiment, LLC
220 East 23rd Street, Suite 600
New York, NY 10010-4658
theexperimentpublishing.com

THE EXPERIMENT and its colophon are registered trademarks of The Experiment, LLC.

The Experiment's books are available at special discounts when purchased in bulk for
premiums and sales promotions as well as for fund-raising or educational use. For
details, contact us at info@theexperimentpublishing.com.

Library of Congress Cataloging-in-Publication Data

Names: Block, Emma, illustrator.
Title: Eat. play. love. : life lessons from my dog / illustrated by Emma
    Block.
Description: New York : The Experiment, [2019] | Text by Michael O'Mara
    Books Ltd.
Identifiers: LCCN 2019030188 (print) | LCCN 2019030189 (ebook) | ISBN
    9781615195947 | ISBN 9781615195954 (ebook)
Subjects: LCSH: Dogs--Pictorial works.
Classification: LCC SF430 .B59 2019 (print) | LCC SF430 (ebook) | DDC
    636.7--dc23
LC record available at https://lccn.loc.gov/2019030188
LC ebook record available at https://lccn.loc.gov/2019030189

ISBN 978-1-61519-594-7
Ebook ISBN 978-1-61519-595-4

Cover design by Beth Bugler
Text design by Claire Cater

Manufactured in China

First printing October 2019
10 9 8 7 6 5 4 3 2 1

DEDICATED TO MY FATHER, PAUL BLOCK—
AND OUR DOG SAMMY (2003–2019)

I've grown up always around dogs. My parents' first dog, Max, was just a few months old when I was born, and when we were both teething, we used to chew books together on the living-room floor. Later in life, my parents got another dog, Sammy, who was the beloved family dog for fifteen years.

Today, visiting my parents always means an excited furry friend meeting me in the hallway, long Sunday afternoon walks on the beach, evenings spent curled up on the sofa together, and an abundance of dog hair on everything. I love dogs and always will. They are eternal optimists, silly, playful, forgiving, and endlessly loyal, which is why we can all learn a little something from them.

—Emma

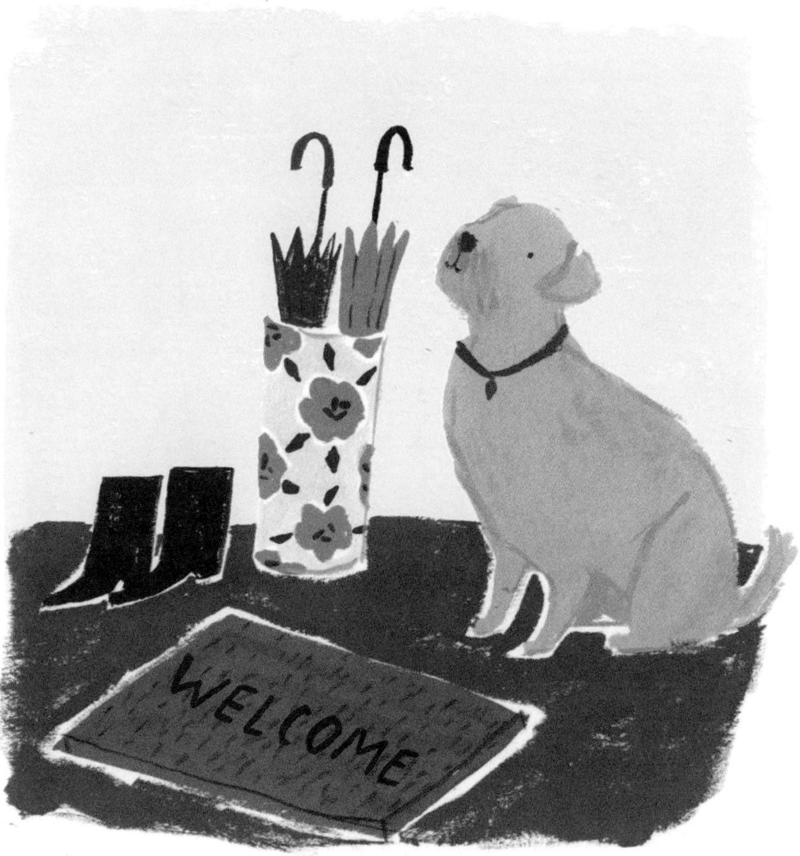
WELCOME

STRETCH EVERY MORNING

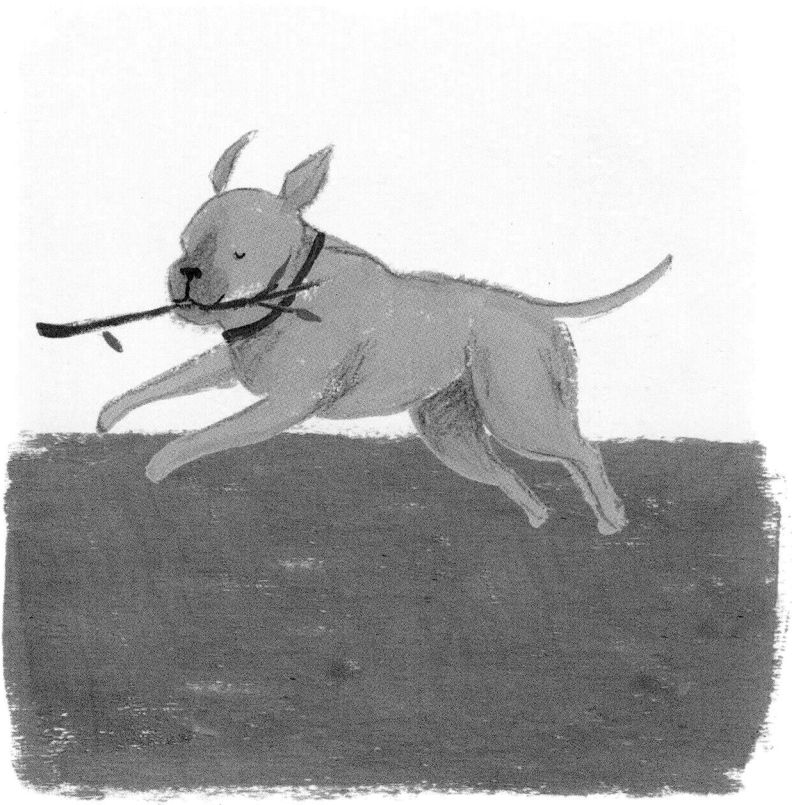

PLAY EVERY DAY

SPEND LOTS OF TIME OUTSIDE

GET ENOUGH SLEEP

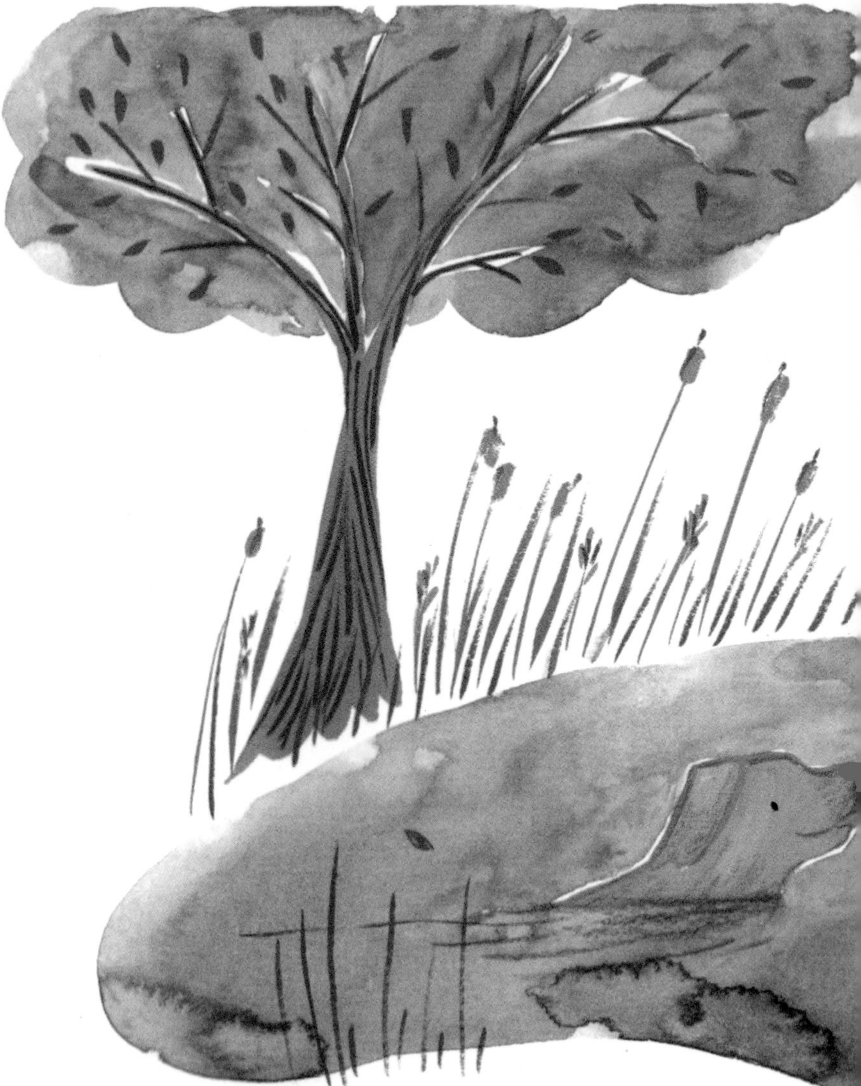

STAY ACTIVE

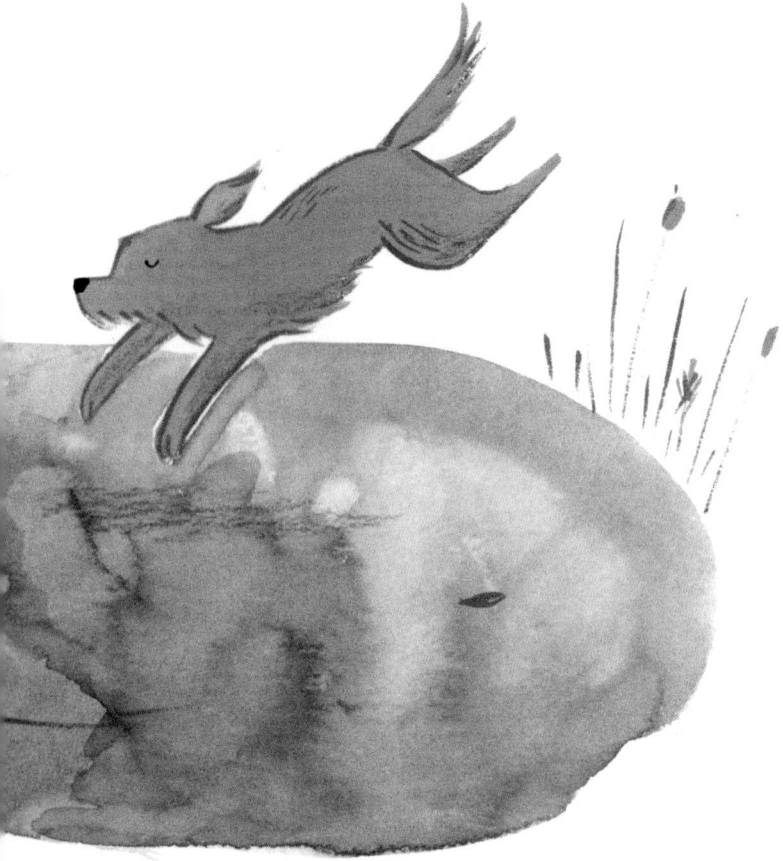

. . . BUT CHERISH

THE LAZY DAYS

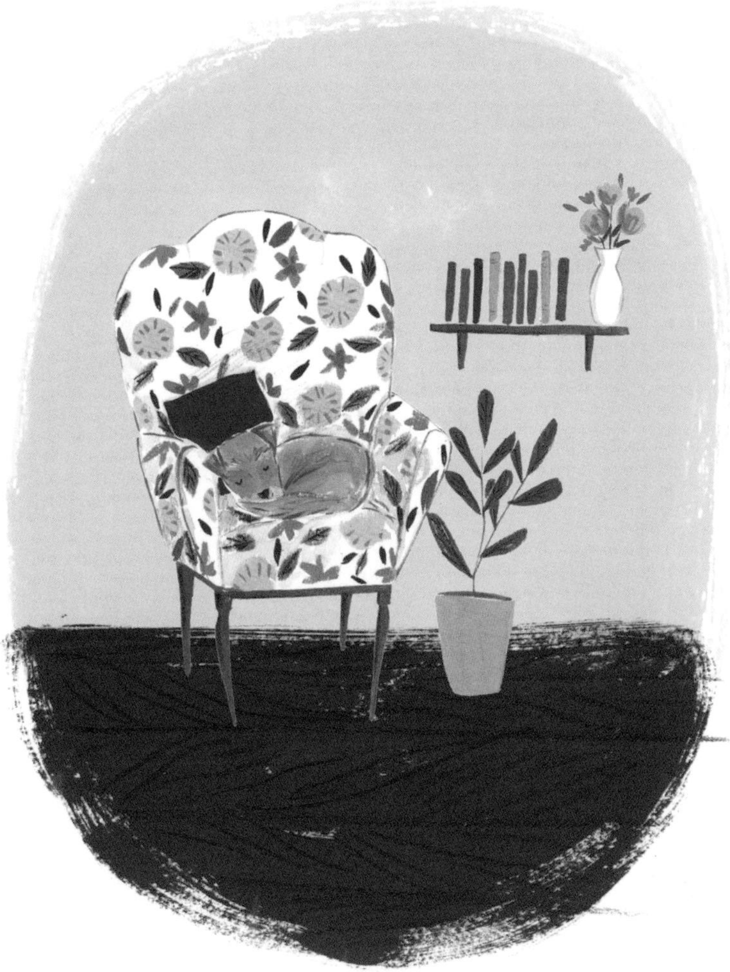

DRINK LOTS OF WATER

SAVOR YOUR FOOD

WALKING IS THE BEST EXERCISE

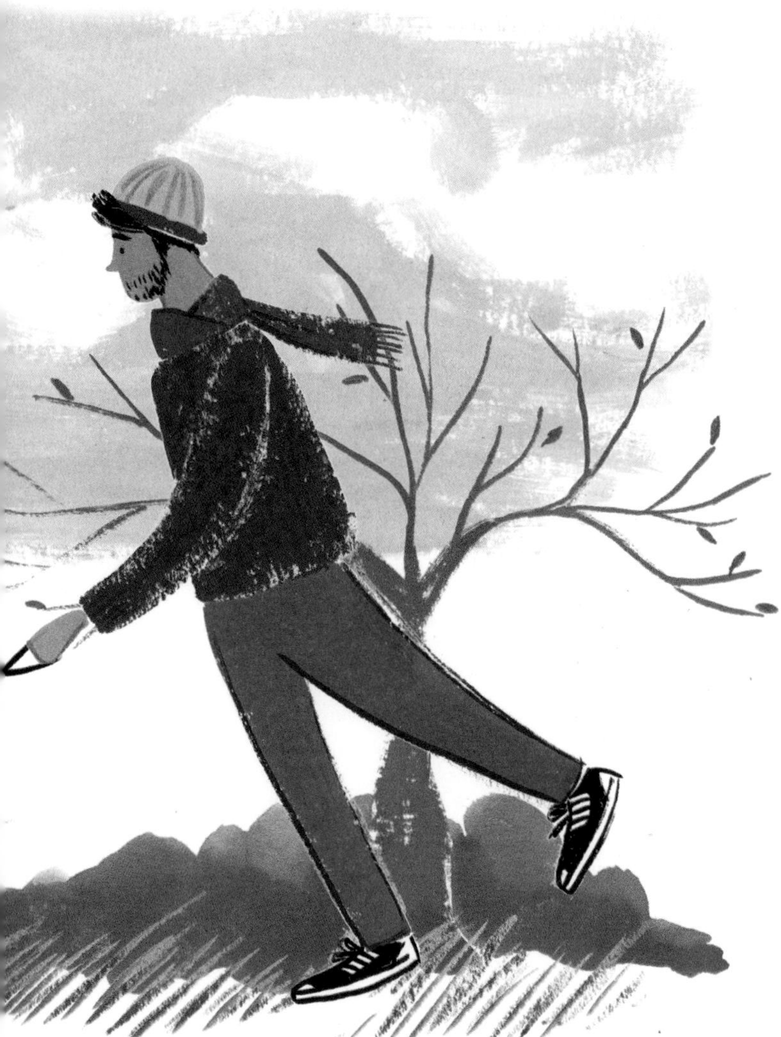

PAWS FOR REFLECTION

WITH PRACTICE, YOU
CAN NAP ANYWHERE

BEING SMALL
DOESN'T MEAN
YOU CAN'T
DREAM BIG

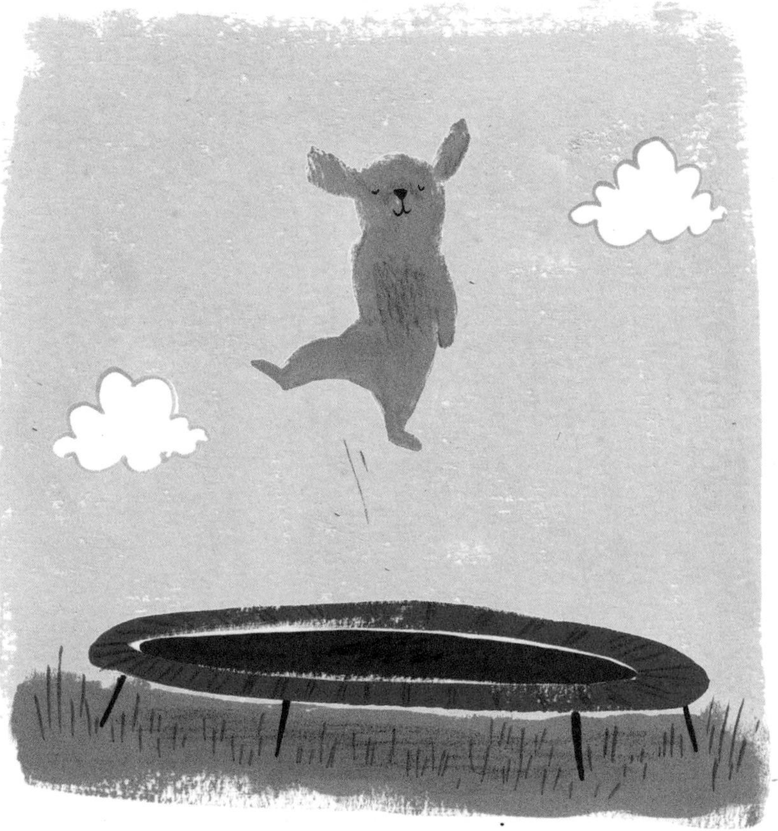

ANY JOB IS WORTH DOING WELL

CHASE THE THINGS THAT
ARE IMPORTANT TO YOU

SEIZE ALL OPPORTUNITIES

MOVE PAST YOUR MISTAKES

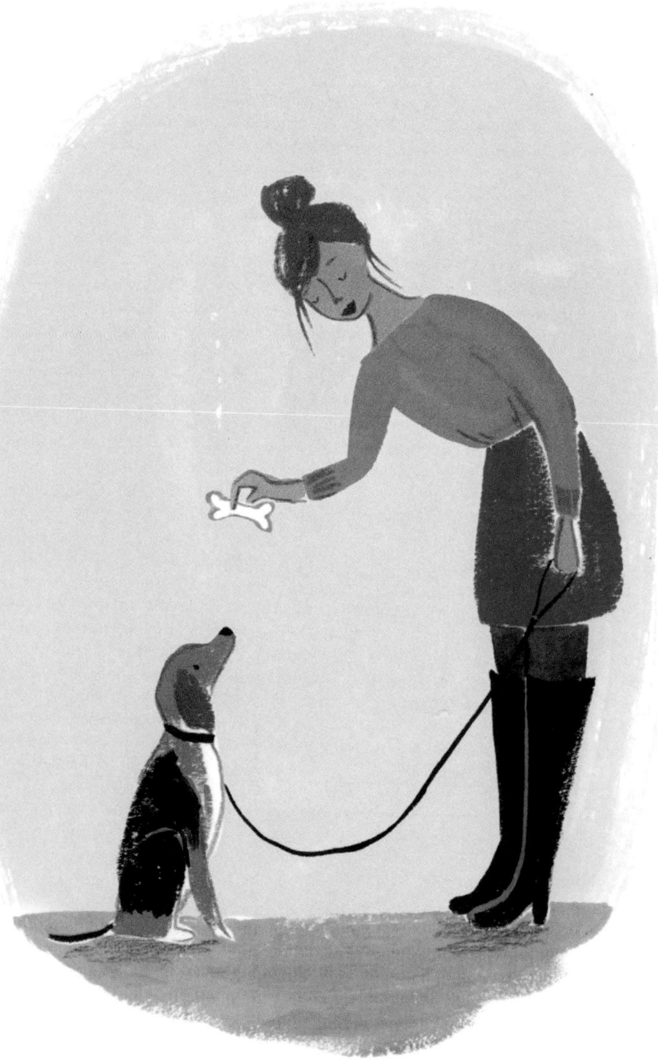

STAY
FOCUSED
ON
YOUR
GOAL

PERSISTENCE PAYS OFF

AND PRACTICE . . .
MAKES . . .
PERFECT!

CARRY YOURSELF WITH CONFIDENCE

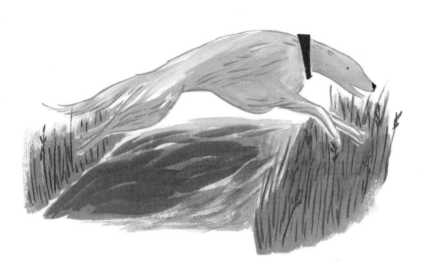

FEEL THE FEAR AND DO IT ANYWAY

DON'T GOSSIP

MAKE YOUR STRONGEST RIVAL
YOUR BEST ALLY

ALWAYS

MAKE EYE

CONTACT

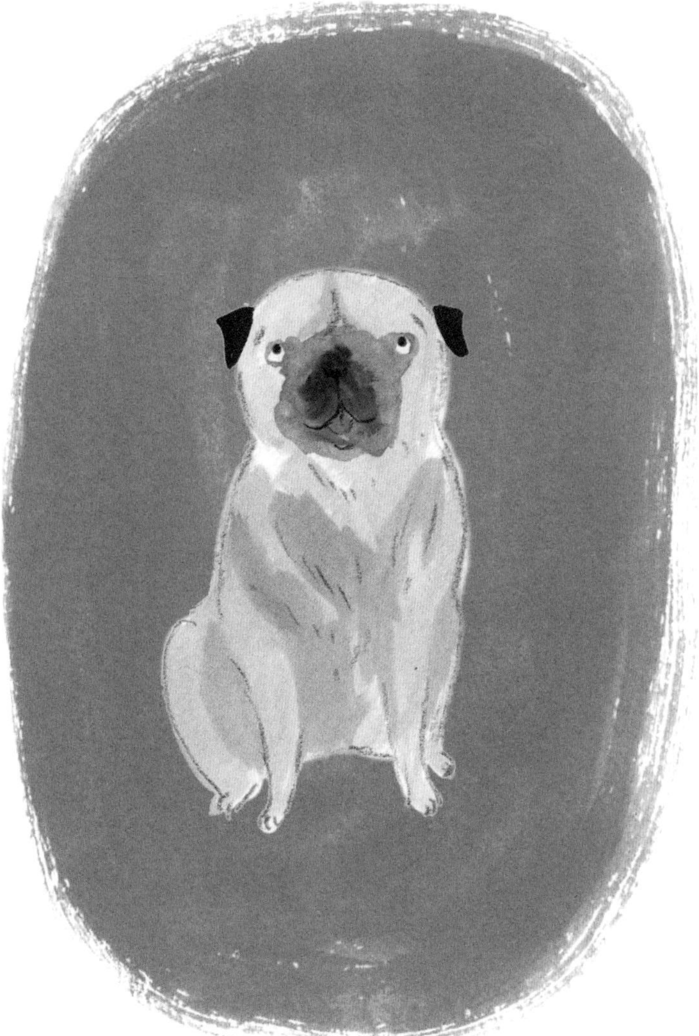

BODY LANGUAGE IS HALF
OF NEGOTIATION

A LOOK CAN BE MORE ELOQUENT THAN WORDS

ACT FIRST, APOLOGIZE LATER

DON'T CONTAIN YOUR ENTHUSIASM

REMEMBER TO TAKE
BREAKS AT WORK

...AND <u>FROM</u> WORK!

DON'T WORRY
WHAT OTHERS
THINK OF YOU

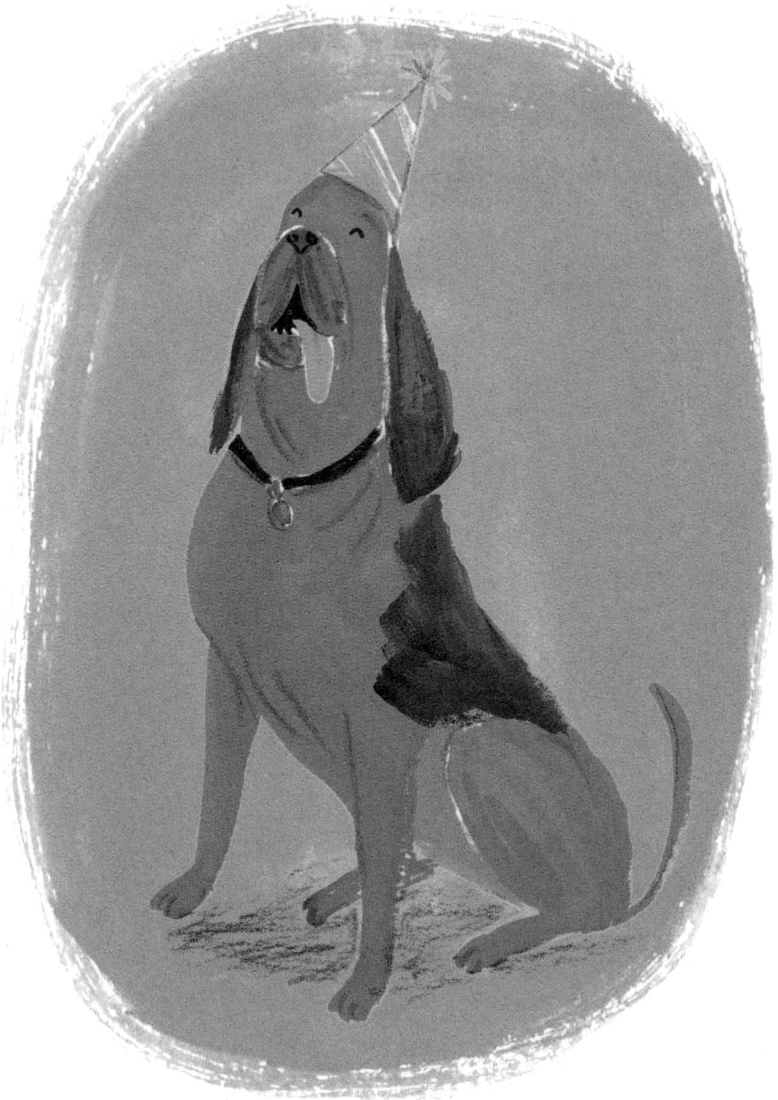

MAKE YOUR NEEDS KNOWN

GROWL WHEN YOU
WANT SOME SPACE

ROCK YOUR

OWN STYLE

. . . BUT SOMETIMES IT'S OK TO BLEND IN

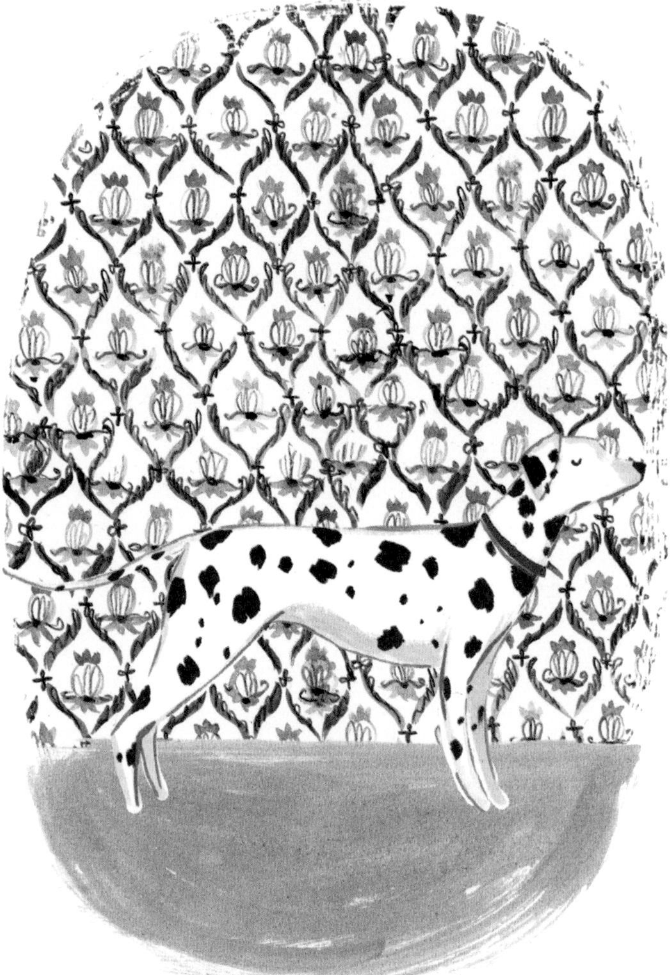

NEVER PRETEND TO BE
SOMETHING YOU'RE NOT

MAKE YOURSELF HEARD

KNOW WHEN TO HOLD OUT FOR
SOMETHING BETTER

ACCEPT COMPLIMENTS

DON'T TAKE YOURSELF TOO SERIOUSLY

DON'T BE AFRAID
TO TAKE UP SPACE

LOOK FOR THE PLEASURES
WITHIN REACH

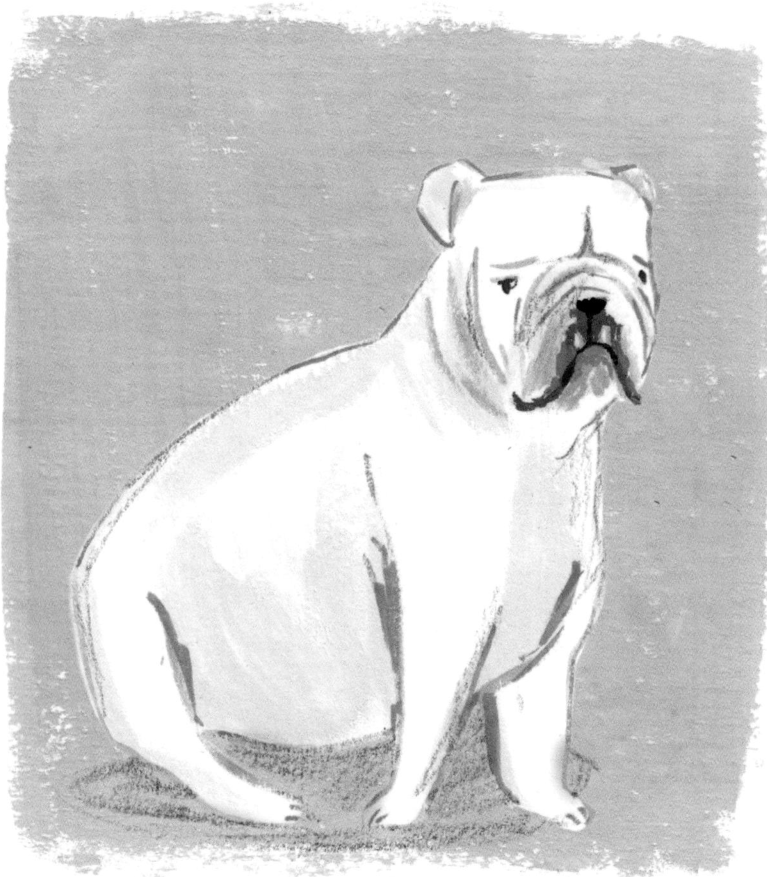

ACCEPT

YOURSELF

TAKE LIFE AT YOUR OWN PACE

YOU YOURSELF HOLD THE
KEY TO CONTENTMENT

STOP AND LISTEN

ENJOY THE JOURNEY

ENJOY THE SILENCE

ENJOY

THE

VIEW!

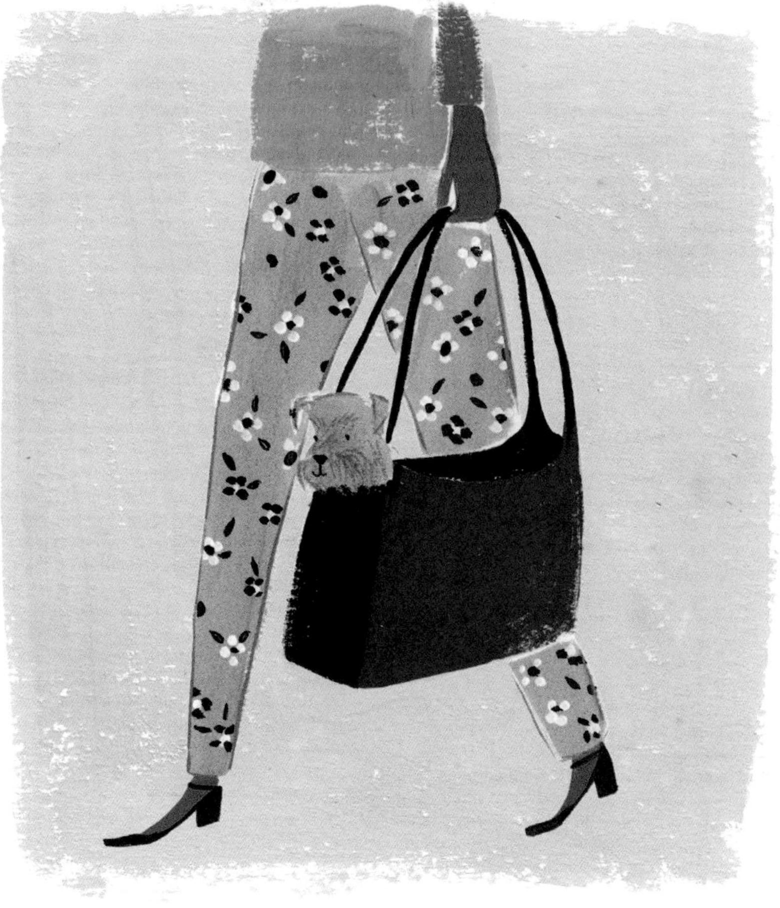

LIVE IN THE MOMENT

. . . BECAUSE YOU ARE THE SUM
OF YOUR EXPERIENCES

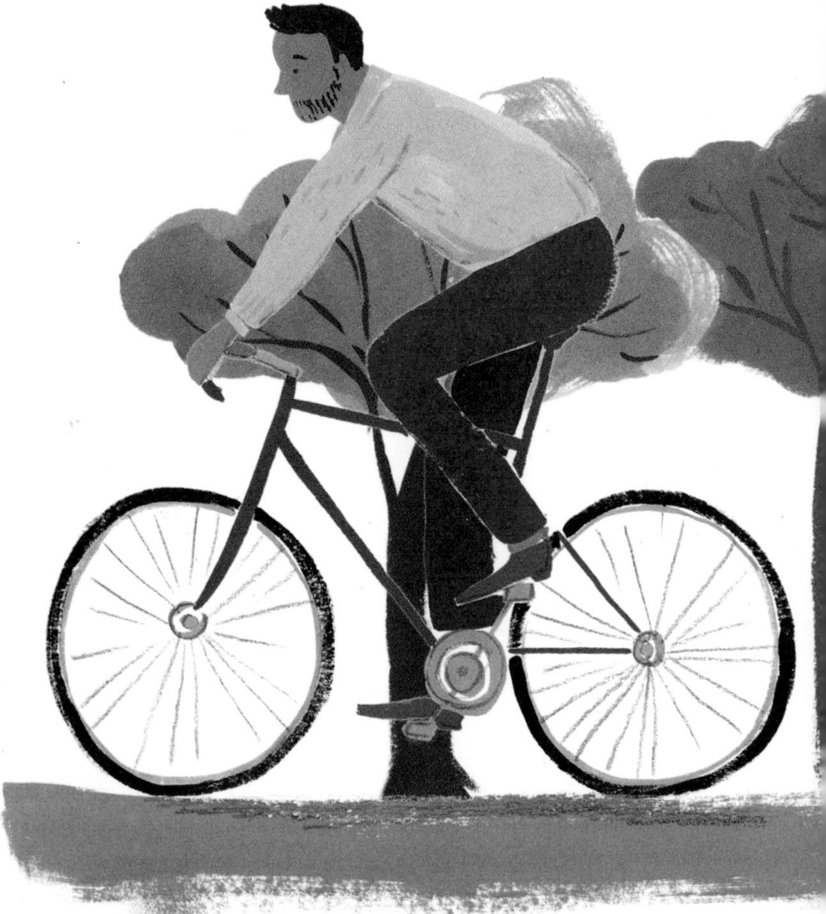

FOLLOW YOUR BLISS

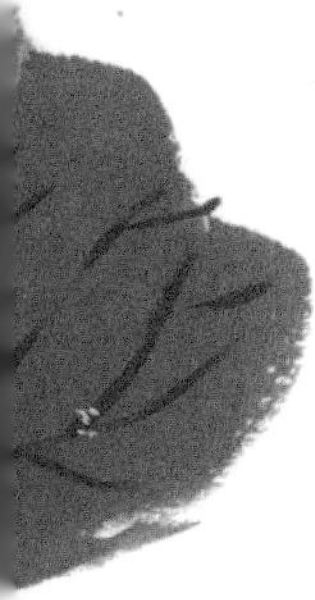

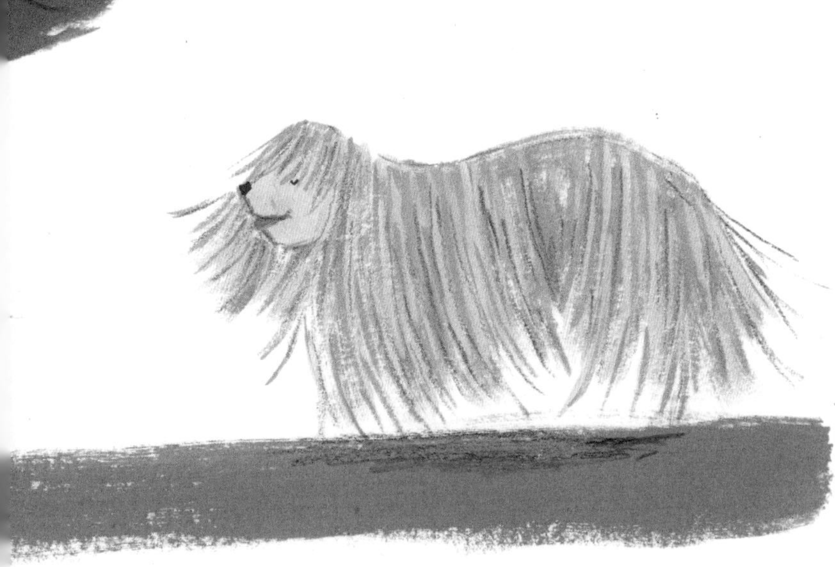

DON'T DWELL ON THE PAST

ACCEPT WHAT'S
BEYOND YOUR CONTROL

BE POSITIVE

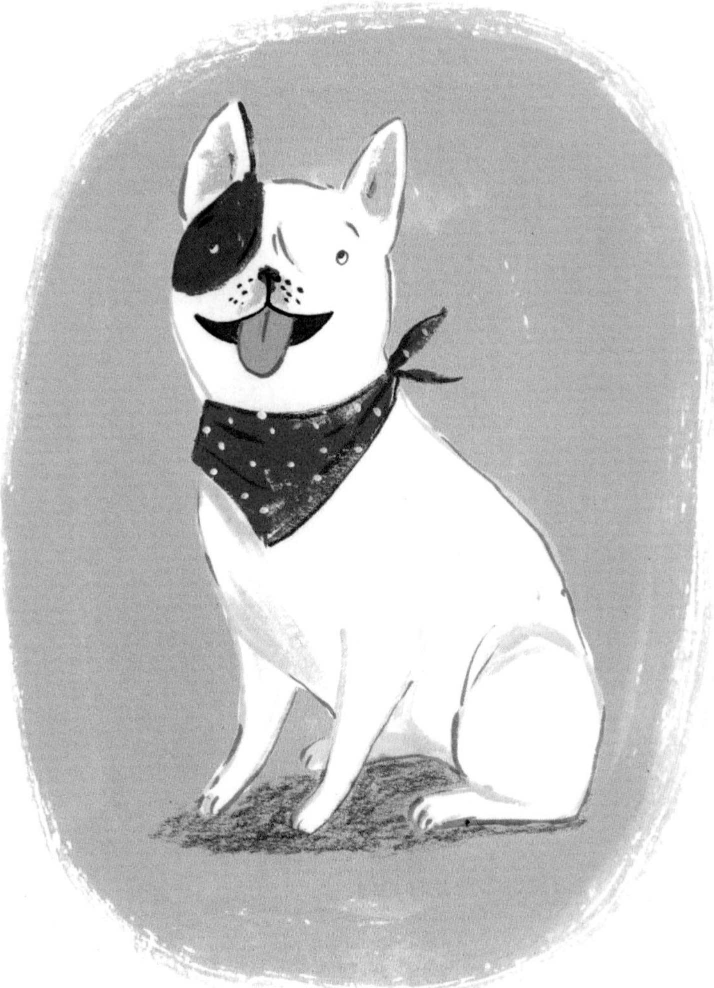

BE TOLERANT

SHOW COMPASSION

EXPRESS INTEREST
IN OTHERS

LOVE WITHOUT EXPECTATION

GREET THE ONES YOU LOVE

DON'T BE AFRAID TO
SAY YOU CARE

LOVE AT FIRST SIGHT IS REAL

THE HEART WANTS
WHAT IT WANTS

LOVE NEEDS NO WORDS

OVERCOME FEAR WITH LOVE

LOVE UNCONDITIONALLY

DON'T JUDGE A BOOK BY ITS COVER

BEAUTY IS IN THE
EYE OF THE BEHOLDER

LOOKS

CAN BE

DECEIVING

VARIETY IS THE SPICE OF LIFE

. . . SO TRY ANYTHING ONCE

DON'T GROW UP

YOU'RE NEVER TOO OLD TO PLAY

STAY CURIOUS

LIFE'S TOO SHORT TO BE SAD

PUT YOURSELF
IN THE PATH OF
OPPORTUNITY

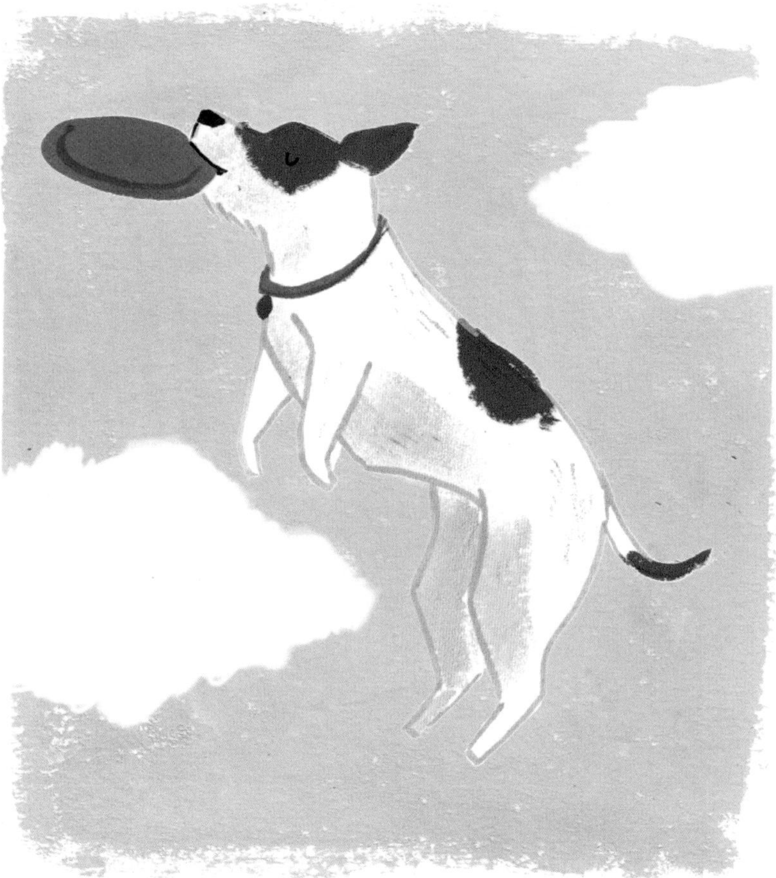

ADAPT TO NEW SURROUNDINGS

BE PREPARED

EMBRACE ADVENTURE

...BUT APPROACH THE
UNKNOWN WITH CAUTION

TOUGH TIMES NEVER LAST

THE SIMPLE THINGS IN
LIFE ARE THE BEST

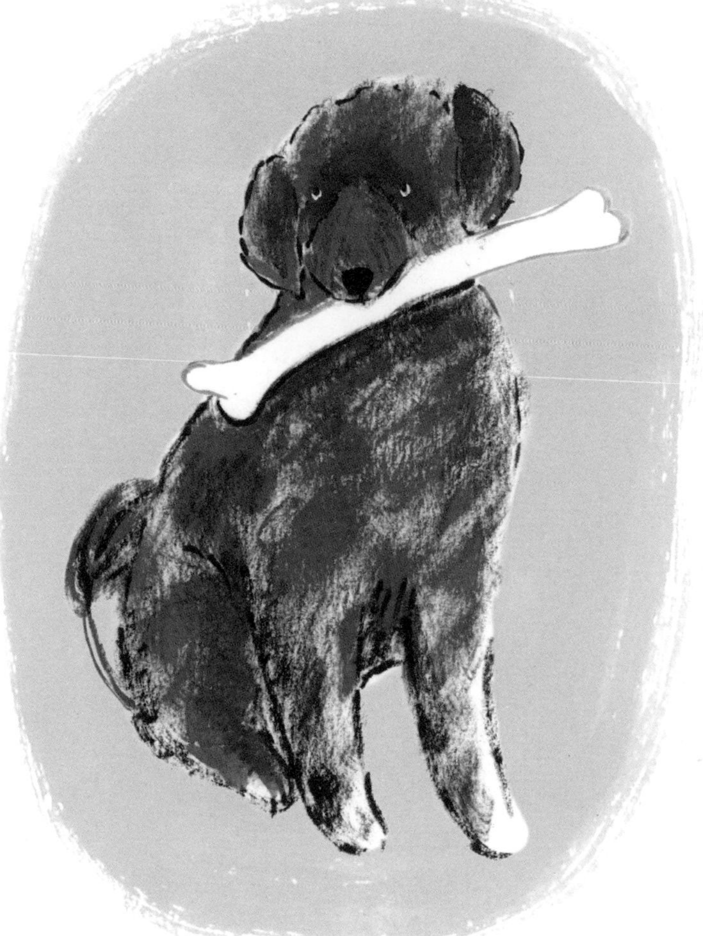

BITE OFF

WHAT YOU

CAN CHEW

PLACE YOUR TRUST WISELY

THERE'S NO SHAME IN
ASKING FOR HELP

TO LISTEN IS MORE IMPORTANT THAN TO UNDERSTAND

FRIENDSHIP

CAN BE EASY

BE LOYAL

SUPPORT EACH OTHER

SHARE YOUR GOOD FORTUNE

... BUT ESTABLISH
YOUR BOUNDARIES

GIVE EVERYBODY A CHANCE

. . . BECAUSE FRIENDS COME IN ALL SHAPES AND SIZES

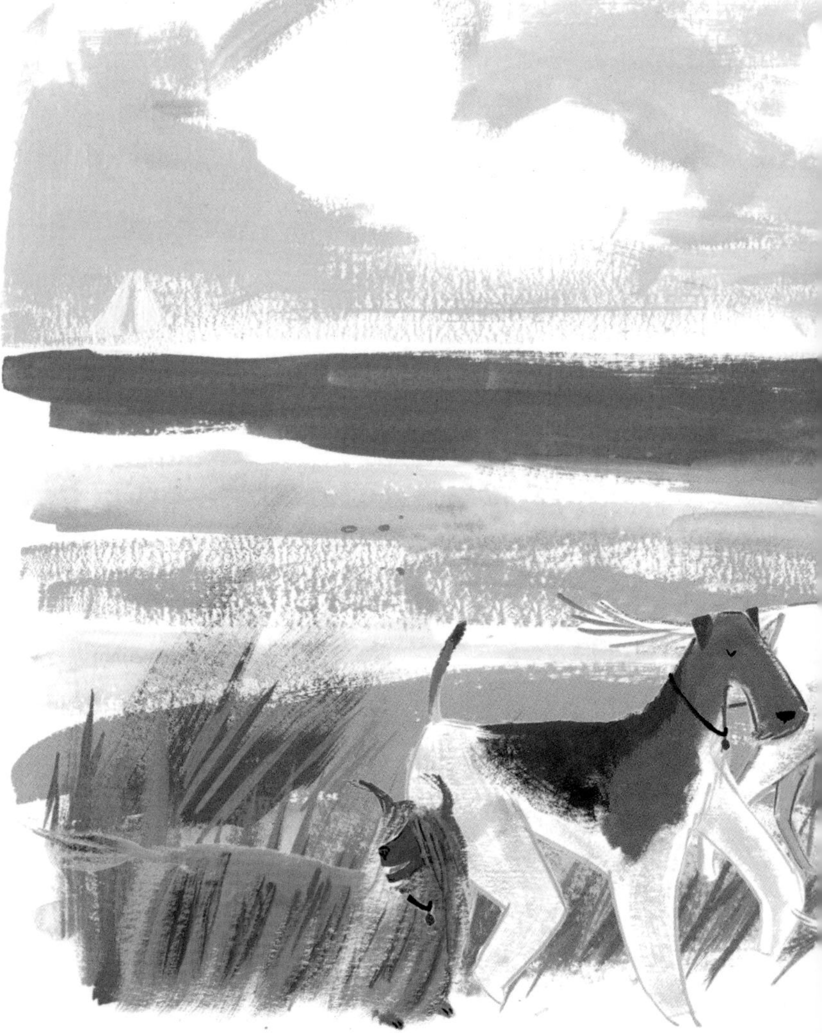

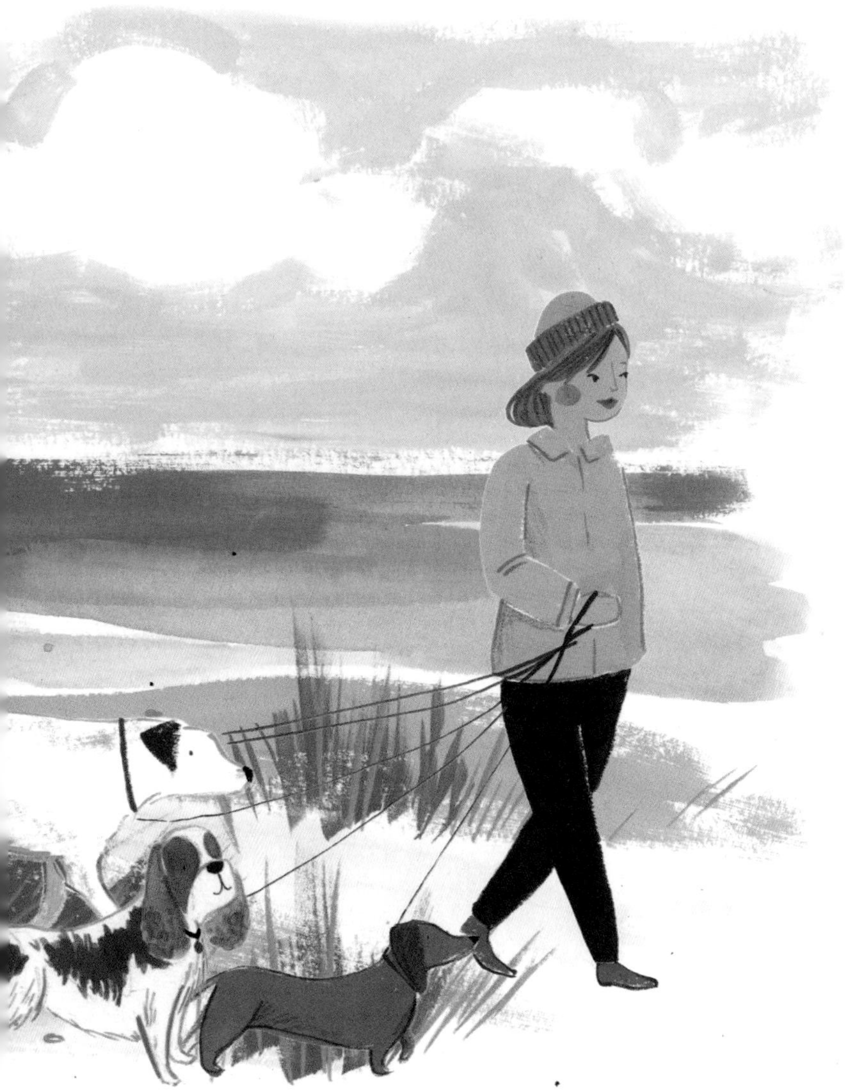

HOLD ON TO EACH OTHER

A BEST FRIEND IS FOR LIFE

WE ARE MORE ALIKE
THAN DIFFERENT

IT'S THE SIZE OF YOUR
HEART THAT MATTERS

NO ONE
IS AN
ISLAND

London artist **Emma Block** creates hand-painted editorial illustrations for brands and publications; teaches watercolor, gouache, and brush lettering workshops; and runs a popular Etsy storefront. Her work is inspired by old photos and films, vintage clothing, travel, 1950s illustration, 1930s jazz, and sausage dogs. She is also the author of *The Joy of Watercolor.*

EmmaBlock.co.uk
emmablockillustration